CONTENTS

CHAPTER 4: KNOWLEDGE AND UNDERSTANDING OF THE WORLD

CHAPTER 5: PHYSICAL DEVELOPMENT

CHAPTER 6: CREATIVE DEVELOPMENT

PHOTOCOPIABLES

INTRODUCTION

Exploring the material

Young children are fascinated both by the world of make-believe and by small objects. Small world play therefore plays a prominent part in their lives, offering them the chance to explore the physical world as well as their own feelings and relationships with other people. Puppets, dolls and play figures can provide the means to escape into a world of fantasy or to act out and come to terms with the daily frustrations of childhood. Models of farms, hospitals and garages, along with their multitude of accessories, can help young children to find out how things work and the way the environment functions.

Whether the equipment is fashioned at home from clothes pegs and cardboard boxes or whether it is sophisticated, commercially-produced models, it is nevertheless, a vital component in a young child's play and development. Always allow ample time for children to play freely and for them to investigate the equipment thoroughly before expecting them to concentrate on more structured activities.

Learning through play

Play is the medium through which young children learn about life in all its many aspects. They are continually investigating and exploring their ever-expanding world and trying to make sense of what they see, hear and feel. The *School Curriculum and Assessment Authority* (SCAA) recognises this fact and has placed great emphasis upon the need for practical and enjoyable activities in the *Desirable Outcomes for Children's Learning.*

Small world play has been designed to meet many of those outcomes by providing activities which extend and enhance children's play in all six Areas of Learning identified in the SCAA document, encouraging them to look at familiar toys and equipment in a fresh and creative way. Using toy vehicles to inspire the creation of music (page 51), for example, will hopefully encourage children to look again at other everyday objects and to question and explore the possibilities for learning that they too might offer.

Setting up the environment

No specialist knowledge or equipment is required to complete the activities in the book which can be undertaken with little preparation beyond clearing a space, gathering the necessary items together and giving initial explanations or instructions. Sometimes you may need to make a demonstration model or some labels before you begin but the basic requirement is just a safe and comfortable learning environment.

Equipment and storage

Small play figures such as LEGO and Duplo and peg dolls can easily be stored in ice-cream or margarine tubs. Label the tubs with words and pictures to allow access to both readers and non-readers. Involve the children in deciding how to sort the figures for storage – whether by type, size or function – and this should encourage them to pack away tidily at the end of the session.

Large models such as dolls' houses and garages can sometimes cause storage problems due to their size and unyielding structure, so consider your storage facilities when you buy such items. Some designs may be more stackable than others or may be versatile enough to serve several purposes. Others may pack flat or fold away for storage.

If storage is a real problem, consider constructing simpler, less permanent models yourself which can be discarded or converted into something else after a few weeks. A few shoe boxes and some play figures when accompanied by a young child's imagination, can become anything from a hospital to pirates' caves. Add animals and trees and it can become a zoo or safari park. And with the addition of vehicles it can be a multi-storey car park, a town or even an airport.

Use a few squares of appropriately coloured fabrics instead of expensive playmats to provide an ocean, a field or a stretch of Tarmac. Children can produce their own road layouts or railway tracks on large sheets of thick paper or opened out cardboard boxes, using pencils, felt-tipped pens or paints. The possibilities are bounded only by your imagination and patience.

Health and safety

Regularly check all small toys to ensure that there are no loose parts which could be swallowed or could trap small fingers. Encourage the children to let you know about any damage or breakages as soon as they occur so that repairs can be carried out or replacements obtained. Check any wooden items for cracks or splinters regularly. Throughout the book you will find a CARE! warning where special caution should be taken.

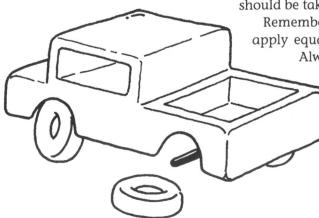

Remember that health and safety matters apply equally to adults as well as children. Always ensure that any toys which are stacked are secure and unable to topple even when touched and always remember not to over-reach when storing or retrieving toys on high shelves. Never stand on anything other than stepstools or stepladders to gain extra height.

Using adult helpers

The presence of an interested adult can help increase a child's concentration, promote and stimulate discussion and extend the vocabulary. It is essential to observe carefully and not to impose your own ideas on the child. Instead, ask open-ended questions to stimulate thought. Listening to the children's answers will give a good indication of their level of understanding and can provide a basis for further questions or suggestions. Accepting a child's answers in a non-judgemental and sensitive manner will encourage and assist rather than interrupt the flow of play. Any praise given should be sincere and deserved – or the child will quickly lose faith in your judgement.

Observation and assessment

It is important to focus the attention during observations in order to assess each child's progress effectively. Keep a note pad and pen nearby to jot down relevant points as they occur. If it is impractical to make even rudimentary notes during observations, then set aside time for this as soon as possible after the activity while details are still fresh in your mind. Important areas for assessment include interest and enthusiasm; concentration and perseverance; ability and willingness to learn; physical, oral and emotional confidence; co-operation; and the ability to initiate and follow through ideas. This list may look rather daunting but it is possible to focus on only one or two aspects at a time during any one observation.

Try to make time for regular periods of close observation of individual children in order to build up a picture of their all-round progress as well as to highlight any difficulties or special skills they may possess. Future activities can then be chosen or adapted to suit individual needs as well as the needs of the group.

Links with home

Always recognise and value the contribution which a child's parents or carers can make to the group. Make a list of anyone who is willing to help in any way – by volunteering as a helper, repairing toys or supplying resources such as wool or cardboard and do call upon that help as soon as the need arises. Encourage carers to try activities they may not at first consider, for example clay or woodwork. If they feel uncertain of their abilities in a particular area, offer them the chance to come in and observe regular helpers at work or consider the possibility of offering them a little on-the-job training to boost their confidence.

Even if carers are unable to take an active role in the group on a regular basis it is important that they should not feel isolated or left out. One way to do this is to encourage

children to use symbols, pictures or letters to make notes to take home to remind carers of particular events, or items you may be collecting. Use copious signs, posters and fly-sheets to keep everyone up-to-date and fully informed about the group's activities. Finally, try to make time to discuss any real concerns or issue genuine praise at the end of every session or send a written message home with the child if you feel the carer is likely to dash away before you have a chance to talk.

How to use this book

Small world play contains six activity chapters, each of which is devoted to one particular area of learning and structured around the headings which are explained below.

Objectives

Although the one main objective mentioned at the beginning of each activity deals with just one area of the curriculum, most activities will also cover several other areas of learning. For example, language development is a constant and continuous process and is therefore implicit in every activity.

Group size

A guide to the number of children who can be involved in the activity with one adult supervisor is given. This can be adapted to suit your circumstances, the number of adult helpers you have and the maturity of the children.

What you need

Everything you need to complete the main activity is listed but again, it can be adapted to suit your circumstances and the availability of materials.

Setting up

Most activities will require an introductory discussion or instruction period. Some of the ideas may also require a certain amount of preparation such as setting out equipment or labelling various items. It is generally a good idea to try out any practical activities yourself, in advance, so that you will be aware of any difficulties or questions that might arise when the children embark upon the tasks themselves.

What to do

The activity is explained from beginning to end, with explicit instructions as well as general suggestions. Illustrations are provided where further guidance may be necessary.

Questions to ask

This section contains some suggestions for the type of questions you may find useful to ask the children. They are intended to prompt discussion and promote further questions and discussion. Remember to allow time for the children to consider and discuss their own questions as well as those posed by the supervising adult.

For younger children

A suggestion for adapting the activity to suit younger or less able children is offered. You may be able to think of further ideas yourself which are more suited to the particular children in your care.

For older children

An extension of the main activity for use with older or more able children is also provided. Encourage these children to think of their own ways to broaden the scope of the activity if they can. This, in itself, is an excellent exercise in creative thinking.

Follow-up activities

Some suggestions are made for extending or broadening the activity to cover other areas of learning and to spark further ideas of your own or of the children.

Photocopiable activity sheets

One activity from each chapter is accompanied by a photocopiable resource sheet to be found at the back of the book. Some of these are used as part of the main activity while others can be used as a follow-up to that activity. The text offers suggestions for ways in which to use the pages. You may wish to enlarge some of them to A3 size to make it easier for very young children.

Topic web

The following page contains a photocopiable web showing all the activities in the book with the relevant page references.

PERSONAL AND SOCIAL DEVELOPMENT

LANGUAGE AND LITERACY

PHYSICAL DEVELOPMENT

MATHEMATICS

SMALL WORLD PLAY

KNOWLEDGE AND UNDERSTANDING OF THE WORLD

CREATIVE DEVELOPMENT

Encourage small world play to develop language skills and word acquisition. Using familiar rhymes and experiences the children can extend their speaking and listening skills and with 'Name train' and 'Musical hats' they can learn to spell some simple words.

HUMPTY DUMPTY FINGER PUPPET

Learning objective
To foster an awareness of the rhythm of words through a popular nursery rhyme.

Group size
Up to four children.

What you need
Paper, pencils, crayons, adhesive, scissors, (a hole punch is useful but not essential).

Setting up
Make a puppet yourself as an example. Use it to illustrate the nursery rhyme Humpty Dumpty, encouraging the children to join you in reciting the rhyme.

What to do
Give each child a piece of paper ($\frac{1}{2}$ A5 size is ample), ask them to draw an oval or egg shape as big as they can and then to cut it out carefully. They can then colour the oval and add facial features. An adult should then cut out two finger holes, about 1.5cm in diameter at the bottom of the body. (Use a hole-punch to make a starting-place to avoid folding the paper.)

Using a scrap piece of paper, show the children how to draw and cut out one arm shape on folded paper to make a pair. Colour the arms in and stick them into position on the back of each Humpty. Encourage each child to use the finished puppet to act out and recite the rhyme.

Questions to ask
Encourage the children to listen very carefully to hear the pattern of the rhyme. Did they notice that the first and second lines had the same pattern? What about the third and fourth lines? Can they hear any words that 'sound the same' or 'rhyme' with each other? Which word rhymes with wall? And what rhymes with men?

For younger children
Let younger children use pre-cut shapes which they can colour and assemble.

For older children
Suggest that they use a small cardboard box to make a wall for Humpty and perhaps write his name on it.

Follow-up activities
● Tap out some other familiar rhymes for the children to guess.
● Use photocopiable page 59 to make a six-piece puzzle.
● Paint a picture of Humpty on his wall, adding sand to the paint for a realistic brick finish.
● Number each piece of the puzzle (photocopiable page 59) and use it with a dice for a 'beetle-drive' type of game.

LAND OF MAKE-BELIEVE

Learning objective
To encourage the
children to create their
own imaginative
stories based on the
theme of dragons.

Group size
Up to four children.

What you need

A sand tray, several 'tyrannosaurus-type' dinosaurs, scraps of red, orange and yellow fabric, play figures, small twigs and stones and some dragon stories, for example *There's no such thing as a dragon*, Jack Kent (Happy Cat Books, Blackie) and *Alexander and the dragon*, Katherine Holabird (Aurum Books for Children).

Setting up

Convert the dinosaurs into dragons by fixing strands of fabric in their mouths to represent flames!

What to do

Read a dragon story aloud to the children and discuss it together. Invite the children to act out the story using the equipment in the sand tray.

After several minutes of play, suggest that the children might like to make a story of their own about dragons. Encourage them to work together and to use and develop each other's ideas. Be ready to help by asking questions if they seem to be struggling with the 'plot' in order to further develop the creative ideas.

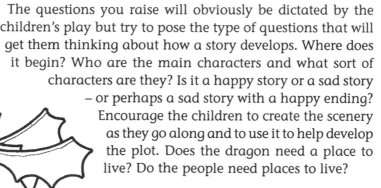

Questions to ask

The questions you raise will obviously be dictated by the children's play but try to pose the type of questions that will get them thinking about how a story develops. Where does it begin? Who are the main characters and what sort of characters are they? Is it a happy story or a sad story – or perhaps a sad story with a happy ending? Encourage the children to create the scenery as they go along and to use it to help develop the plot. Does the dragon need a place to live? Do the people need places to live?

For younger children

Start the story off yourself, for example 'Once upon a time there was a very lonely little dragon...' and ask the children for ideas to continue the story while you narrate and they enact it.

For older children

Invite them to make a zigzag book of the main events in their story, using pictures and/or words so that others can enjoy it later.

Follow-up activities
● Use the children's story as the basis of a drama session.
● Tape record the children telling their story so that they can develop it further at a later date.
● Depict the story in a group-painted wall frieze.
● Find out about other mythical creatures such as unicorns and minotaurs.

NAME TRAIN

Learning objective
To help children learn to recognise their own names.

Group size
Up to six children.

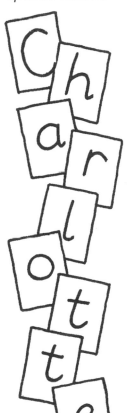

What you need
Blu-Tack, off-cuts of card 6cm × 4cm, toy engines and carriages. A name card for each child is useful but not essential.

Setting up
Print either a lower or upper case letter on each card to give sufficient cards to spell out the names of the children in your group.

What to do
Ask the children if anyone thinks they can spell their own name. Invite a volunteer to try to find the letters of their name from those available. (Use a name card with the child's name on to refer to if necessary.) Look at each letter as it is found and make its sound as you trace over the shape for all the children to see.

Attach this name to the toy train with Blu-Tack, beginning with the capital letter which can be stuck on the engine. Explain that it is a very important letter which is called, for example 'Em' for Michael. Attach each subsequent letter of the child's name to its own carriage to complete the train. Once the entire name is spelled spend some time discussing it before moving on to the next child and so on until all the names are spelled. Line up the trains and again discuss what you can see.

Questions to ask
Are all the trains the same length? How many letters are in the longest train? Whose name is on the shortest train? Are there any letters the same as each other? What are the letters on the engines called? (Capitals.) Why are they important? (Because they begin the names.) Can you find your own name-train? Can you find your friend's?

For younger children
Construct only two trains at a time for comparison of length.

For older children
As each letter is selected invite all the children to trace its shape in the air as you talk them through it, for example, 'round, up and down – that says 'a' (as in apple)'.

> **Follow-up activities**
> ● Muddle the carriages of a name train and invite its owner to reconstruct it.
> ● Race the trains across the floor by holding up a letter and allowing only the trains which contain that letter to move forward one space on a paper track until they reach a 'station' at the end.
> ● Make a collection of toy trains to discuss and compare.
> ● Make junk model trains.

FAMILY COLLECTIONS

Learning objective
To aid recognition of letters by shape and sound.

Group size
Up to four children.

What you need
A play figure for each child, various objects beginning with different letter sounds, a bag.

Setting up
Decide which letter you wish to work on and label each play figure around the middle with it. Make sure you have plenty of objects beginning with that sound, as well as several which do not.

What to do
Place the objects in the centre of the table and hand out the play figures, one per child. Go through the objects to make sure the children are familiar with them, pronouncing each item's name clearly, placing particular emphasis on its initial sound. Now put all the objects in the bag.

Introduce the letter on the play figures, saying, for example that it is a letter 'ess' and it says 'sss'. Explain that the play figures must each try to collect as many objects as they can that start with that sound. Let the children take turns to select an object from the bag and decide whether it fits the criterion or not. Those which do can be kept in front of the child and those which do not can be given back to you.

Questions to ask
As each object is pulled from the bag ask the children if it begins with, for example, 'sss'. If they are not certain, ask what the item is and repeat the sound clearly again. For example if you have a 'pig' ask – does 'pig' begin with 'sss'? If the children are still not certain ask 'Is it a 'sssig'? (Hopefully, they will laughingly agree that it is not!)

For younger children
Label the objects with their initial sound so the children can visually as well as aurally match them.

For older children
Let older children work independently, by giving each child a different letter to work on.

Follow-up activities
● Put the objects in the centre of the table and race to collect three correct ones.
● Draw or paint as many objects as you can beginning with the chosen sound.
● Put a number on the play figure's back and allow the children to search the room until they find the right number of objects beginning with the chosen letter.
● Make letters using phonically appropriate materials, for example an 'a' with apple pips', a 'b' with buttons, 'c' with cotton, 'd' with dough and so on.

MUSICAL HATS

Learning objective
To aid recognition and matching of simple words.

Group size
Two to 20 children.

What you need
A selection of soft toys, each with a hat to fit (paper ones are sufficient), pens, paper, a cassette player and music tape.

Setting up
Write the name of each toy – 'teddy', 'baby doll', 'hedgehog' – clearly on the toy's hats and on labels for the toys' tummies. Sit the children in a circle and put the soft toys in the centre. Spend a few moments introducing each toy and reading its name from the label and the hat. Remove the hats.

What to do
Tell the children you are going to play some music and while it is playing they must pass a hat which you will give them around the circle. When the music stops, the child who is holding the hat must find the toy whose hat it is and put the hat on. If the child is correct, the child chooses another hat to be passed around. If not, pass the same hat around again. Play continues until all the hats are correctly placed on their owners' heads.

Questions to ask
Encourage the children to look at the word on the hat as they pass it round. If they are not sure what it says what could they do? (Look at the names on the toys to find one the same.) When a child wrongly matches a hat to its owner, suggest they look at the first letters on the toy and the hat. Do they match? Allow the children time to self-correct. Reinforce the correct match once it has been made.

For younger children
Use the children's own names on the toys and hats.

For older children
Have no name labels on the toys, only on the hats.

Follow-up activities
● Play the game using other familiar words rather than names.
● Make up some alliterative sentences about each toy, for example, 'Teddy took ten tigers to tea'.
● Have a toys' tea party, making place labels, using the named hats and setting a table with relevant play crockery and cutlery.
● Play other musical games such as pass the parcel and statues.

WHATEVER HAPPENED TO YOU?

Learning objective
To encourage the fluent expression of thoughts.

Group size
Up to 20 children.

What you need
A selection of play figures, Dri-marker pens, small pieces of white fabric.

Setting up
Using the Dri-marker pens and white fabric, give each play figure a different injury, for example a black eye, a bandaged head, a sling or mud all over.

What to do
Show one of the play figures to the children and invite them to suggest what might have caused the figure's disability. Encourage all the children to contribute. Once all the ideas have been exhausted, move on to the next figure and again invite suggestions. Encourage the children to speak in whole sentences and prompt them to give you clear explanations. Discuss the probability of the various ideas actually occurring if the children seem to be moving into the realms of fantasy.

Questions to ask
Have the children ever had any of the injuries depicted themselves? How did they happen? What was done about them? Has any child ever been to hospital for an X-ray? Can they explain to the group what happened? Remind the children to keep themselves as safe as possible by thinking carefully all the time about what they are doing.

For younger children
Be sensitive to the fact that some children could become upset if painful memories of injury are rekindled.

For older children
Discuss emergency procedures such as what to do in the event of a fire and how and when to dial 999.

Follow-up activities
● Read *On the Way Home* by Jill Murphy (Macmillan).
● Make a hospital for play people using small boxes to make beds, trolleys, wheelchairs and ambulances.
● Learn to correctly name the different parts of your body.
● Have your dominant arm put in a sling for 15 minutes to see how difficult it is to draw or paint with your other hand.

TEDDY'S GOING SHOPPING

Learning objective
To encourage the communication of meaning by use of words and symbols.

Group size
One or two children at a time.

What you need
Empty grocery cartons, play fruit and vegetables, teddy bear with a shopping bag, paper and pencils.

Setting up
Set up a small area of the room to represent a shop, using the cartons and play greengrocery.

What to do
Introduce the teddy bear to the children and tell them that he is going to the shops but he keeps forgetting what he has to buy. Ask them to suggest what they can do to help him remember the six things that he needs.

Then allow the children to take turns, in ones or twos, to first compile a shopping list and then to accompany the teddy bear to the 'shop' to collect the required items. Let them show you the shopping for checking along with their list.

Questions to ask
Talk about shopping trips which the children have made with their parents or grandparents. Have they ever forgotten anything? Do the adults ever take anything to help them remember what they need? (Hopefully someone will mention a list.) Adults usually write out their lists but what could the children do if they were not sure how to write everything down? (Draw pictures.) How could they check that they have got all the items on the list? (Tick them off as they go along or cross out each item as it is bought.)

For younger children
Suggest that they fetch only two or three items to begin with.

For older children
Suggest that they take the teddy bear to the shop with his list and leave him there until the shopkeeper has filled his basket for him. (This means that the list they have compiled must be deciphered by the shopkeeper.)

Follow-up activities
● Read *Don't Forget the Bacon* by Pat Hutchins (Picture Puffin).
● Draw a shopping basket for each child, with the words 'Teddy bought...' printed at the top and invite them to draw or write what he bought inside the basket.
● Extend the activity by pricing the goods in pence and giving teddy a budget of fifteen pence.
● Take teddy and his list on a real shopping trip – perhaps for ingredients needed for a cookery session.

BABY'S BEDTIME

Learning objective
To encourage the enjoyment of books.

Group size
One or two children at a time.

What you need
A dolls' cot or bed, a doll, a selection of familiar story books and some comfortable chairs or beanbags.

Setting up
Make a cosy corner for the doll to go to bed in and place the chairs/beanbags close by the bed.

What to do
Discuss bedtime and all it entails together. Let the children talk about their own experiences and practices. Invite the children to take turns to put the 'baby' to bed and to read it a story, while you quietly observe the action. Note how the children handle the books and whether they use the illustrations to help their 'storying'. Listen to their intonation and watch their facial expressions. These observations will provide a good indication of the children's progress along the road to independent reading and also of their verbal skills.

Questions to ask
Invite the children to describe their own bedtime routine. Is it the same every night? Or does it sometimes vary, for example, at weekends or when they have visitors to stay? Do they have a favourite story that they like to be read again and again? Who, if anyone, does read them a story? (Dad, Mum, sister, brother.) Or do they look at a book or listen to a tape themselves instead?

For younger children
Make sure your selection of books contains plenty of familiar picture stories to help them 'read' with confidence.

For older children
Set up equipment to tape the children 'reading' to the baby.

Follow-up activities
● Extend the activity by adding a baby bath, towel, hairbrush, toothbrush and a change of clothes for the doll.
● Make a set of routine bedtime activity cards for the children to put into sequence.
● Read *Peace at Last* by Jill Murphy (Macmillan).
● Choose six well-known stories and conduct a survey to show which is the most popular.

CHAPTER TWO

Activities to develop children's mathematical skills such as sorting and number recognition are explored in this chapter. In 'Picnic time' children can learn some simple geometric shapes and in 'People patterns' they can copy some ordering patterns.

WHOSE DINNER?

Learning objective
To encourage logical thought to solve a problem.

Group size
Up to ten children.

What you need
A set of dolls or play figures, toy food items, small paper plates, off-cuts of cardboard, felt-tipped pens.

Setting up
Choose an item of food for each play figure which you are going to pretend they dislike. Draw a picture of that food on a piece of cardboard and cross it out. Sit the figures in a line and prop their 'dislike label' up in front of them.

What to do
Gather the children together so that they can all see the figures and explain that their labels are showing us which food they do not like. Spend a few minutes going through the labels and making sure every child understands their meaning. Then tell the group that you are going to make up a dinner for one of the toys and they have to try to work out who it is for. Take a paper plate and place on it all but one of the items shown on the cards, thus making it suitable for only one of the toys. Invite the children to suggest whose dinner it might be.

Questions to ask
Remind the children to look at the toys' labels and to think carefully. Encourage them to work systematically to eliminate each toy in turn. What does the first toy dislike? (Peas.) Are there any peas on the plate? (Yes.) So would he like this dinner? (No.) What about the second toy?

For younger children
Reduce the number of toys to two at a time for comparison.

For older children
Introduce multiple dislikes: for example carrots and peas.

Follow-up activities
● Encourage further discussion by using different forms of the same food. For example, if someone does not like potatoes does that mean he won't like chips?
● Use play dough to make up favourite dinners on paper plates.
● Play 'What's the time Mr Wolf?'.
● Hold a food-tasting session using some unusual or exotic foods.

HAPPY FAMILIES

Learning objective
To learn a sorting game using play figures.

Group size
Up to four children.

What you need
Four different sets of play figures, each consisting of four people with a common characteristic, for example: all made of wood, all wearing yellow, all with jointed knees, all wearing hats (if you can't find four suitable figures, adapt some to suit your purposes by adding a blob of paint or a sticker), a bag to contain the figures.

Setting up
Introduce the figures to the children and make sure they can recognise the common characteristic for each family. Let the children each select a family to collect during the game.

What to do
Put all the figures into a bag and let the children take turns to dip in to select a figure. They must look at the figure they have picked out and decide whether it is one of their chosen family or not. If it is, the child can then keep it, if not they must put it back into the bag, and play passes to the next child, continuing until everyone has collected a complete family of four.

Questions to ask
Encourage them to give a reasoned justification if they can keep the play person, 'Yes, it belongs to my family because it has a hat.' If the child is not sure, ask what was special about the family. (They all wore hats.) Does this person have a hat? (Yes.) What does that tell us? (That it belongs to my family.)

For younger children
As each figure is withdrawn from the bag it can be given to the appropriate child rather than returned to the bag, thus shortening the game.

For older children
Introduce two characteristics for the families such as, they all have jointed knees and hats, or add some extra figures to the bag which don't belong to any of the families.

Follow-up activities
● Draw or paint each member of your own family on a house-shaped piece of paper to build up a street scene.
● Learn to write the names of all the people who live in your house.
● Find out the correct names for different baby animals.
● Invent a sorting game of your own, using a bag and some small toys.

MOVING HOUSE

Learning objective
To encourage the development of sorting and classification skills.

Group size
Initial introduction and discussion – whole group. One to four children for the task.

What you need
Two dolls' houses, boxes and furniture for each room of the house, a lorry or truck to contain the boxes, pens and pencils.

What to do
Position the two houses at a distance from one another so that the lorry can travel between them. Show each piece of furniture to the children, encouraging them to name it, describe its function and suggest in which room it might belong.

Discuss the meaning of 'moving house' and encourage the children to think about ways in which the furniture could be sorted and packed to move from one house to the other most effectively. Hopefully, someone will come up with a valid solution such as putting all the furniture from one room into the same box. That child can then be invited to demonstrate this idea to the whole group. Once several ideas have been suggested and demonstrated, small groups of children can then complete the task during the activity session.

Questions to ask
How will you know where the boxes belong when they arrive in the new house? (Encourage the children to come up with their own ideas for labelling – with numbers, colours, pictures or words.) Different people have different names for various rooms for example lounge/sitting room/front room or study/office/den, and for various items of furniture such as sofa/settee or footstool/buffet. So explore these differences to ensure that each child understands fully.

For younger children
Restrict the furniture to a few basic items and be ready to help with the labelling of the boxes.

For older children
Suggest that older children draw a map to help the lorry driver get from one house to the other.

Follow-up activities
● Draw simple plans to show the layout of various rooms.
● Use a house-shaped piece of paper and old catalogue pictures to make a collage of the furniture in various rooms.
● Describe a piece of furniture and let the children try to guess what it is.
● Use some furniture as the subject of a still life painting.
● Use the photocopiable activity on page 60 to sort the items into their appropriate rooms.

NUMBERED ROUTES

Learning objective
To encourage number recognition.

Group size
Up to four children.

What you need
Cars, pens, large sheet of paper (a model house, station, school are useful but not essential).

Setting up
Label each car with a different number on its roof. Draw a maze of roads, each numbered – at the beginning and at every junction – to match one of the cars. At the end of each route place or draw a different destination such as a house, a park, a school or the seaside.

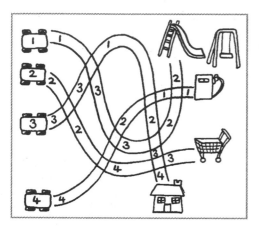

What to do
Challenge the children to find the right route for each car by following the numbers on the roads. Warn them to 'drive' carefully and remind them to stop and look at each junction. Explain that a junction is where roads meet and spend a few minutes letting the children find them on the map.

Questions to ask
Why must you look carefully at each junction? (So that you can see the numbers on the road.) What would happen if you followed the wrong numbers? (You would end up at the wrong destination.) How do real drivers know which way to go? (They use maps and signposts.) Do the children know that real roads have designated numbers? (They may have heard various motorways referred to by number.)

For younger children
Use a much simplified maze such as the one shown.

For older children
Invite them to record the destination of each car in a chart so that it can be used as a check sheet by other children.

Follow-up activities
● Look at road maps and atlases and try to follow different route numbers.
● Draw a maze of your own for others to follow.
● Go for a walk outside and see where you can spot numbers being used, for example doors, gates, road signs, shops, fire hydrants and car number plates.
● Investigate real road junctions and look at the road markings and what they mean.

WHO LIVES NEXT DOOR?

Learning objective
To encourage ordering and sequencing of numbers to ten.

Group size
One to ten children.

What you need
Ten boxes, ten play people, pens, adhesive, paper.

Setting up
Make a paper door for one end of each box, line the boxes up to represent a street and number the doors – from left to right, one to ten. Number the play figures one to ten.

What to do
Spend several minutes looking at the row of houses and their numbers, making sure the children are familiar with them and are aware that the numbers are in order from left to right. Then show the group the play figures and tell the children you are going to see how clever they are at guessing where each person lives.

Hold up each figure randomly and invite a child to find the correct house for it. Work through the figures one by one until they have all been correctly matched to their houses. Then remove them and repeat the procedure, this time hiding the numbers on the play figures and asking more demanding questions. Invite children to place the figures in the appropriate houses.

Questions to ask
I live next door to number 1 so where do I live? I live between number 5 and number 7 so where do I live? My house comes before number 8 so where do I live? My neighbour lives at number 10 so where do I live?

For younger children
Use just five houses and five play people.

For older children
Arrange the houses with odd numbers along one side and even ones opposite them as often happens in real life.

Follow-up activities
● Extend the activity by turning around one or two houses and asking the children to say which numbers they are – or muddle them for the children to re-order.
● Encourage the children to learn their own addresses and telephone numbers.
● Take the group for a walk around the neighbourhood to see who can read the door numbers.

PEOPLE PATTERNS

Learning objective
To encourage recognition and recreation of patterns.

Group size
Up to ten children.

What you need
Various sets of matching play people or small creatures.

What to do
Make a long line of people in a simple pattern for example boy, girl, boy, girl, boy, girl and so on and ask the children if they can see anything special about the line. Hopefully, someone will come up with a suitable answer and you can reinforce this by agreeing that they are in a pattern which goes boy, girl, and so on.

If no relevant answer is forthcoming work along the line touching each figure and saying aloud 'boy, girl, boy, girl', until someone does give the correct answer. Once the pattern is established, invite a child to place the next figure in line to continue it until all the relevant figures are used. Repeat the activity using a different pattern which you can start and ask a child to finish.

Questions to ask
What do the children notice about some of the figures in the line? (They are the same as each other.) How many figures are the same as each other? What do they notice about the remaining figures in the line? (They are also the same as each other.) It may be necessary to remove or lie down the first set to help the children concentrate on those that are left.

For younger children
Before starting the activity spend some time looking at the figures and discussing their similarities and differences.

For older children
Use more complex patterns, perhaps using three or four elements or use figures which vary only slightly from one another.

Follow-up activities
● Invite the children to record some of the patterns you have made by drawing or painting them.
● Suggest that the children might like to devise patterns of their own.
● Invite the children to line themselves up in some sort of pattern, go for a short walk indoors or out, and see if they can keep in that pattern all the way.
● Look for repeating patterns on walls, clothing or floors.

FAMILY CIRCLES

Learning objective
To encourage sorting and counting.

Group size
Two to four children.

What you need
Four sorting rings or hoops, four different play people families (each comprising different elements: one parent, two children; two parents, three children and so on), 32 small objects – eight red, eight yellow, eight blue, eight green, a dice, small sticky labels, marker pen.

Setting up
Use the sticky labels and marker pen to convert the dice to show either the digit '1' or '2' on each face. Give each member of each family a distinguishing feature such as a coloured dot on their tummy.

What to do
Introduce the children to each family and explain that they like to collect things that are the right colour for them. Select an object from your collection and ask the children if they can guess which family it belongs to. Do this several times to ensure that each child understands that the red family collects red objects and so on. Then give each child a hoop and invite them to choose a colour to collect in it. Allow them to select one of their family members to put in the hoop to start them off. The game can then proceed by each child rolling the dice in turn and collecting the relevant number and colour of objects to go in the circle. The object of the game is to collect eight relevant items. Encourage the children to continue playing until everyone has completed the task.

Questions to ask
Who has the most items? Who has the fewest items? Has anyone collected all their family members yet? Which family has the most people in it? How many more objects does each child need to collect?

For younger children
Limit the items to collect to just five each.

For older children
Convert an additional dice to show addition and subtraction signs so that the relevant number of objects must be collected or returned as appropriate.

Follow-up activities
● Invite the children to invent their own collecting games using different criteria.
● Encourage the children to draw or paint a picture of the people who live in their house.
● Conduct a survey to see how many people live in each child's house.
● Play the traditional Happy Families card game.

PICNIC TIME

Learning objective
To familiarise the children with simple geometric shapes.

Group size
Up to four children.

What you need
A few soft toys, a small tablecloth, a paper plate for each toy, an assortment of cardboard, tracing paper, adhesive, scissors, paints, pens and reclaimed materials.

Setting up
Take each paper plate and clearly draw on it three different geometric shapes – select from circle, square, rectangle, diamond, triangle. Place the toys on the floor around the edge of the tablecloth and give them each a plate.

What to do
Gather the group together to see the picnic scene which you have 'discovered'. Suggest that the toys seem to be waiting for something and ask the children what that might be. Once the idea of a picnic is established, take up one plate and say that there seems to be something missing. Hopefully, food will soon be suggested and you can discuss what might fit the shapes on the various plates. Invite the children to make suitable cakes, biscuits and sandwiches using the materials available. The children can then sort them onto the toys' plates.

Questions to ask
How do we make a sandwich? (By putting something between two pieces of bread.) How can we make sure the food will fit the shapes on the plate? (Trace the shapes or make a template.) Encourage the children to name each shape and introduce them to interesting words such as 'parallelogram' as well as the more simple 'diamond'. Which shapes have straight sides? Which are curved?

For younger children
Provide templates of the shapes and make sure that the materials you have available are suited to the task.

For older children
Use less familiar shapes such as hexagons, pentagons, semi-circles and ovals.

Follow-up activities
● Make some real sandwiches and have a real picnic.
● Take a trip to a supermarket and look at the shapes of biscuits and cakes.
● Sort a basket of shopping by shape.
● Put a selection of shapes into a bag and try to guess which is which by feeling them.

CHAPTER THREE

Ideas in this chapter encourage children to share toys together, to work together to solve problems and to care for belongings. Use 'All change' to help children develop their perseverance skills and 'Nativity cones' to link with a Christmas project.

TYRE TRACKS

Learning objective
To encourage children to take turns and share fairly.

Group size
Six children.

What you need
Six small vehicles with different wheel track patterns (choose from: tractor, lorry, bicycle, wheelbarrow, train, car, bus), six shallow trays with thin sponge to fit inside, paint, paper.

Setting up
Mix six different colours of paint and pour a little into each of the trays and place the sponge on top to use as a printing pad. Place the trays in the centre of the activity table and put a vehicle in each tray. Give each child a sheet of paper.

What to do
Demonstrate to the children how to press a vehicle onto a sponge pad so that paint sticks to its wheels and then how to use it to make interesting trails all over the paper. Encourage them to look carefully at the trails to see the different patterns. While the children work at making their own trails encourage them to use different colours and different vehicles working alongside each other.

Questions to ask
What should you do if someone else is using the colour you want? (Ask if you may have it next please.) What could you do while you were waiting for your turn? (Watch what others are doing/use a different colour/look at your own picture and think about where your next trail might go.) What should you do if someone else asks for the colour you are using? (Tell them they may have it as soon as you have finished your trail.)

For younger children
Have a maximum of four vehicles (and only four children) in each group.

For older children
Suggest that older children work in pairs to make a more interesting trail.

Follow-up activities
● Repeat the activity outside, using large wheeled toys and water rather than paint.
● Sharing a magnifying glass with a friend, go with an adult in search of some tracks – from footprints to pushchair tracks.
● Print patterns using different objects and ask a friend to guess which objects you used.
● See how many things you can see where two children are sharing over a ten-minute period, for example, books, toys, food and chairs.

BUILD A ROAD

Learning objective
To encourage children to work together as a group.

Group size
Two to six children.

What you need
Pieces of strong card roughly A4 size, a destination building for example a zoo, hospital or railway station. A few small vehicles, building bricks, a copy of the Highway Code and three garages (converted shoe boxes will do).

Setting up
Talk about roads and the way they are laid out. Explain that a junction is where two or more roads meet and that sometimes two roads will merge into one. Look at the various junctions that are shown in the Highway Code.

What to do
Place the garages at three different points around the room and put the destination building somewhere between them. Give the children the bricks and cardboard and challenge them to build a road system that will enable cars from each garage to drive to the given destination. Remind them that they must work together so that the roads will join, cross and sometimes merge with one another just like real roads.

Questions to ask
What should we do if two people have different ideas about where to put the road pieces? (Talk about it and try to come to some agreement.) Should the same person be allowed to decide every time there is a disagreement? (No.) How else could a decision be reached? (You could take turns to be the decision-maker.)

For younger children
A lot of sensitive adult assistance will probably be needed to help encourage co-operative work with younger children.

For older children
Encourage the children to develop their ideas and to work together to make imaginative use of the bricks by building fly-overs, bridges and roundabouts.

Follow-up activities
● Photograph the completed layout to use as plans for any future road builders to follow.
● Chalk a road layout outside for the children to drive around on wheeled toys.
● The Highway Code contains rules to help adults share roads safely – think of some rules to help children share toys safely (take turns, ask politely for a turn, don't keep one toy for a very long time).
● Read *Mr Gumpy's Outing* by John Burningham (Picture Puffin).

HELP!

Learning objective
To encourage children to work together as a group to solve a simple problem.

Group size
Two to four children.

What you need
A container of water (a baby-bath for example), a round washing-up bowl or similar (small enough to fit inside the water-container leaving space all around), small wood off-cuts, Plasticine, household junk materials and a few play figures for example Duplo people.

Setting up
Invert the bowl in the water to form an island and place the play figures on the island.

What to do
Tell the children that the people have somehow got stranded on an island and it is too far for them to swim safely back to shore. Show them the materials available and invite them to find a way to transport the figures ashore without getting wet. The one rule is that the play figures themselves may be touched only while they are on dry land. Encourage the children to share their ideas with one another, stand back and be ready to provide assistance if required.

Questions to ask
How many different ways are there to cross water without getting wet? (On a bridge, in a boat, by aeroplane, in a bosun's chair for example.) What sort of materials need to be used to travel on water? (Waterproof.) How could you move a small boat without touching it? (Blow it.) How do real boats move? (Sails, engines, oars.)

For younger children
Younger children may have very inventive ideas but will probably need considerable practical help to utilise them effectively.

For older children
Encourage them to write or dictate a story explaining how the people came to be stranded.

Follow-up activities
● Make a scrap-book of water transport, using pictures from magazines, catalogues and newspapers.
● Use a very large cardboard box to make a play boat.
● Look at maps and atlases and try to spot lots of islands.
● Find out about creatures that live under the sea.

WHAT'S GONE WRONG?

Learning objective
To encourage children to treat property with care.

Group size
Up to 20 children.

What you need
A selection of broken and battered toys.

What to do
Look carefully at each toy in turn, allowing the children time to examine each one and to discuss what might have happened to it and how the breakage might have been avoided. Ensure that the children realise that you are not trying to apportion blame as these are very old toys that were broken a long time ago. You may trigger off a confession or two however, so be ready to deal with such an occurrence with sympathy and understanding.

Questions to ask
How can we keep our toys safe when we are not playing with them? (Put them away in a drawer or cupboard.) What should we do if we break something? (Tell someone straight away and apologise.) Try to explain that it is much better to take care not to break things in the first place because however much we apologise it won't mend the breakage. Discuss the idea of 'preciousness'. Is it wise to let someone else use something we consider very precious? Is it wise to borrow someone else's precious possession? What should we do if we find something broken? (Show an adult so that it can be mended if possible.)

For younger children
Be aware that young children may become upset by painful or embarrassing memories of any recent breakages they may have caused.

For older children
Discuss ways of apologising other than just words – a cuddle, a special card or letter or offering a compensatory gift, for example.

Follow-up activities
● Read and discuss *Dogger* by Shirley Hughes (Red Fox).
● Some toys are meant to come apart so that they can be put back together again. See how many different ones you can find – jigsaw puzzles, construction toys, stacking toys and so on.
● Make a Humpty Dumpty finger puppet (see page 11).
● Visit a shoe mender to see how shoes are repaired.

NATIVITY CONES

Learning objective
To enable children to respond to a major event in the Christian calendar.

Group size
Up to four children.

What you need
White paper, crayons, felt-tipped pens, scissors, adhesive, hair-coloured wool, coloured tissues, paper doilies, glitter, photocopiable page 61 for each child.

Setting up
Familiarise the children with the Nativity story and explain that you are going to make models of the characters so that they can be used by everyone to act out the story later.

What to do
Give each child an activity sheet and ask them to think about which character they are going to make – king, shepherd, inn-keeper, angel, Joseph or Mary. When they have chosen their character encourage them to colour each of the three pieces on their sheet appropriately, adding wool for hair or beards. For an angel, make wings rather than arms using two quarters of a doily and add glitter instead of colouring in.
  Once the pieces are ready the children can cut them out and assemble them, using a piece of coloured tissue as a head-dress. When sufficient figures have been made, the children can take turns to use them to re-enact the Nativity.

Questions to ask
How do the children think Mary must have felt after her long journey? What do they think it might have been like in the stable? What about the sounds and smells? Would it have been light in the stable? Where would the little light there was have come from? What lights our homes at night?

For younger children
Younger children could construct sturdier figures using ready-made cones of strong cardboard and scraps of material for clothing.

For older children
Older children could label the characters with an identifying initial or name. They may also wish to depict the story sequentially in the form of a zigzag book adding one scene on each page.

Follow-up activities
● Make some scenery and perform the Nativity play with the figures for others to watch.
● Turn the dressing-up corner into Bethlehem with robes, head-dresses and a 'manger' full of straw.
● Paint a picture of God. (An adult could write down any ideas expressed by the children as they work and display this alongside the finished paintings.)
● Find out about as many different animal homes as you can.

ALL CHANGE

Learning objective
To encourage concentration and perseverance in learning.

Group size
Up to 15 children.

What you need
A selection of small world toys, a screen or cloth to cover the toys.

Setting up
Introduce the toys to the children, looking at them one by one and talking about what they are and what they look like. Make sure the children are all familiar with the name of each toy, particularly if it is a little unusual – such as a submarine, yacht or kaleidoscope.

What to do
Sit the children in a circle and arrange the toys on the floor in the centre. Then tell the children to look carefully at the toys and try hard to remember where they are because you are going to move some and see if they can tell you which ones you have changed. Under cover of the cloth or screen, swap two toys over. Uncover the toys and ask who can tell you what you have moved. Once the children are familiar with the game they can take turns to be the toy mover.

Questions to ask
Why is it important to hide the toys while they are being moved? (To stop the game being too easy.) How can we help ourselves to notice which toys change places? (By looking extra carefully at them before they are covered up.)

For younger children
Use toys that vary considerably from one another.

For older children
This simple game can be made extremely difficult by increasing the number of toys that are used, choosing toys that are very similar to one another and moving several toys rather than just two.

Follow-up activities
● Play the game on a large scale by replacing the toys with children who can stealthily change places while the others close their eyes.
● Invent similar games of observation and concentration for example hide small toys under flower pots then shuffle them around and ask the children to tell you what is under each pot before you lift it up.
● Learn some magic tricks that involve sleight of hand.
● Watch a magician at work and see if you can spot how the tricks are done.

WHAT CAN WE PLAY?

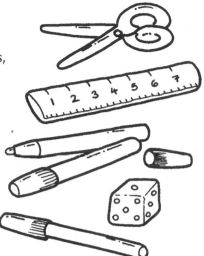

Learning objective
To encourage children to initiate ideas of their own with given equipment.

Group size
Up to six children.

What you need
A variety of small world toys, household junk materials, a selection of manufactured boxed games, adhesive, scissors, felt-tipped pens, rulers, dice and spinners.

Setting up
Introduce the various boxed games to the group and talk about how they are played and what their purpose is. Then suggest that the children might like to make up some games of their own – in pairs or individually – that they can play later with friends.

What to do
Show the children the materials you have available and then stand back to observe their efforts and to supply any extra materials they may request. As they work, encourage them to explain what they are trying to do and be ready to assist if they are becoming frustrated by their own efforts. Suggest that they test their finished game out amongst themselves before letting others play it so that refinements can be made if necessary.

Questions to ask
What sort of a game is it? (A collecting game, a race, a building game?) How will it be played? How will it end? Will there be a winner? How many people will be able to play? How will other people know how to play it? (Offer to write out any rules they make up, to keep with the game.) How can the pieces of the game be kept safely together? (They may wish to find a suitably sized box to decorate and label.)

For younger children
Suggestions may be necessary to start them off – play people might race along a track to get home first, cars may have to be pushed or guided along a track using a straw and avoiding obstacles such as trees, houses and people.

For older children
Encourage attractive presentation of their game and suggest that they may like to write out their own rules.

Follow-up activities
● Invite parents to join in a games afternoon, using a selection of both bought and home-made games.
● Conduct a survey to find out which was the most popular game played.
● Make a display of all sorts of indoor games.
● Find out about indoor games that were played by parents or grandparents when they were young.

FEELINGS

Learning objective
To learn about the
expression and
acceptance of a range
of moods and feelings.

Group size
Up to 15 children.

What you need
A selection of play figures and accessories, an open-sided dolls' house or cardboard box room.

Setting up
Think of several minor accidents which occur almost daily for example spilt milk, wet pants, knocked down tower of bricks, painting ruined by spilt paint and so on. Arrange the play figures and accessories inside the house to depict one of these accidents.

What to do
Gather the children around to view the scene and discuss what they think has happened and how the person involved might feel. Then remove the figures and set up another situation to discuss.

Questions to ask
What has happened? (Someone has spilt paint all over the little boy's picture.) Has this ever happened to any of the children? Can they remember how they felt at the time? (Upset/angry/sad/ disappointed.) And how did this make their body feel? (Hot/tearful/ wobbly.) What did they do about it? (Shouted/cried/told an adult.) What might have made them feel better? (A hug and a kind word/ help to clean up the mess/an apology from whoever spilt the paint – even if it was an accident/ help to re-do the picture.) Explain that we all get these sorts of feelings sometimes for many different reasons and we should try our best to help someone who might be upset.

For younger children
Try to keep discussions light and positive and be aware that they might trigger the recall of past upsetting events.

For older children
Invite them to set up the figures into situations familiar to themselves.

Follow-up activities
● Make simple masks using paper plates on sticks, with the two sides showing two opposite moods (happy/sad, cross/ pleased, worried/ carefree, shy/ confident).
● Sing 'When you're happy and you know it clap your hands', making up extra verses about different moods – 'When you're angry and you know it shake your fist' for example.
● Use old magazine and newspaper pictures to make a collage of different moods.
● Mime different feelings for other children to guess.

Help children find out about the world in which they live through play, with a look at roads, railways, airports, hospitals and farms. In 'Where we live' and 'Garages' they can also explore the details of their immediate surroundings.

SLEDGES AND SLOPES

Learning objective
To undertake an investigation into the slipperiness of a variety of materials.

Group size
Up to six children.

What you need
Play people, small pieces of rigid plastic, different types of cardboard, felt, sandpaper, a selection of fabrics (such as corduroy, silk and satin), plastic lids, tin lids, small wooden bricks and planks, unbreakable mirrors, white fabric.

Setting up
Cover a table top with white fabric to represent snow and put all the other materials on a surface nearby.

What to do
Explain to the children that the table can be used as a sledging area for the play people and that they can use the available materials to make their own slopes and sledges. Talk about steep and gentle slopes and ask the children to think hard about which would be the best slope for sliding down. Encourage them to feel the various materials with the palms of their hands to try to assess their slipperiness. (Remind them to test the fabrics in all directions since results might differ considerably, for example on corduroy.) Suggest that they test the different lids for slideability too – on the flat fabrics as well as on slopes.

Questions to ask
What happens if the slope is too steep? (The people fall out of their sledges.) What if the slope is too gentle? (The sledges won't move.) If a slope is covered with felt can the people sledge down it? Why not? Do the mirrors make good slopes? Can anyone explain why this is? What about the sandpaper and the different types of cardboard? Are there any other materials that might be suitable?

For younger children
Provide ready-made slopes covered in various materials for the children to explore.

For older children
Encourage them to record their findings in ways they think might be suitable for other children to understand.

Follow-up activities
● Investigate ice and find out whether it is always slippery. For example will ice slide down slopes made of felt?
● Use coloured ice-cubes for some colour-mixing activities.
● Use some sandpaper to smooth offcuts of both soft and hard woods.
● Visit a playground with a slide and investigate its slipperiness, for example by sitting on a coat or putting the soles of your shoes down as you go, or seeing how the materials of different clothes affect it.

TAKE ME THERE

Learning objective
To learn about the
purposes of various
features of the
environment.

Group size
Up to six children.

What you need
A road layout showing various features such as park, post-box, shop (commercially produced playmat or a home drawn layout), play people (adults and children), a small bag containing a letter/postcard, a ball, a shopping list and any other items connected with the features shown on your particular layout. A small house for each child.

Setting up
Ask the children to sit around the edge of the playmat and give each child a play adult and child. Point out the various features on the layout one by one and discuss their purpose. Then talk about the items in the bag and what they might be for. Choose a site for each child's house and tell them to put their play people in their houses.

What to do
Invite each child in turn to dip a hand into the bag and pick out an object. The child must then guide the play people from their house to the relevant feature. So, if the child picks out a letter then the people must go to the post-box, if a ball is selected then they must go to the park and so on. Encourage the child to talk about the route as the play people travel to their destination. Use this opportunity to continually remind children not to wander off or cross roads without an adult's hand to hold.

Questions to ask
Can you see the destination you are heading for? Can you see the safest way to go? Where might be a safe place to cross? (Pelican crossing, zebra crossing, footbridge or lollipop person.) What do you pass *en route* to your destination?

For younger children
Use a much simplified layout and be ready to help talk them along their route.

For older children
Let older children work in pairs, with one giving the other directions to follow.

Follow-up activities
● Use photocopiable page 62 to reinforce the idea of following a route.
● Visit the nearest post-box and watch it being emptied.
● Tell the group about a place you have visited and describe some of the things you saw there.
● Draw a picture line to show the things you passed to get here today.

RAILWAYS

Learning objective
To discuss and observe a feature of the wider environment.

Group size
Up to 15 children.

What you need
Pictures, posters, books and models of trains, display cases (upturned plastic fish tanks are suitable), toy train sets, pencils, paper, crayons, paints.

Setting up
Display posters and pictures and arrange both fiction and non-fiction books in an interesting and accessible way. Place any precious model trains in display cases at a suitable viewing height and those less precious on open view. Put the train sets on table tops or on the floor nearby.

What to do
Gather the group in front of the display and ask the children to tell you about some of the things they can see. Then choose one item to look at more closely. Talk about it and encourage questions to be asked and comments to be made. Invite children to choose an item they would like to know more about and again observe and discuss it within the group. Ask the children to add to the display by bringing in suitable things from home. (Remind them to have them carefully named.)

Stand back and let the children play with the train sets, explore the display and paint or draw pictures. Be ready to answer questions, share books and generally encourage the children to discover more about trains.

Questions to ask
Has anybody been on a train? What did it sound like as it travelled along? Most trains today are electric or diesel-driven but they used to be mostly steam. Has anyone seen a steam train? Are there any pictures of steam trains in the display? How can we tell it's a steam train?

For younger children
Look at the display in groups of only three or four to enable every child to ask questions and contribute.

For older children
Add a box of bridges, stations and trackside houses.

Follow-up activities
● Build a long train with big cardboard box carriages.
● Visit a railway station and listen to the sounds of the passengers, the announcers and the trains.
● Sing 'She'll be coming round the mountain'.
● Make a very long train mural by having each child paint a carriage.

THE AIRPORT

Learning objective
To talk about journeys and past events.

Group size
Up to six children.

What you need
An airport layout (commercially produced or home drawn), play people, aeroplanes and helicopters of different sizes and types, wheeled vehicles including a fire-engine and an ambulance, a large flat building or box with a removable roof, a passport, maps, atlases and globes.

What to do
Sit the group around the layout and talk about what you can see. Encourage the children to use technical terms such as departure lounge, checking-in desks, cock-pit, pilot, control tower and runway. Invite any children who have travelled by aeroplane to tell the group what happened and what they did. Show them the passport and see if they know what it is. Then invite the group to play with the layout whilst you observe and be ready to answer questions, supply extra equipment, help to find different countries on the atlases and continue to provide technical words and explanations.

Questions to ask
Why do we need aeroplanes? (Because they can travel long distances, at speed, over land and sea.) Who flies aeroplanes? (Pilots. Remember to point out that these can be male or female.) Where does the pilot sit? (In the cock-pit.) What does the pilot wear? (A uniform.) Who else wears a uniform? (Nurse, soldier, schoolchild and bus driver for example.) Why do the children think these people wear uniforms?

For younger children
Limit the size of the group to four and take a more active role yourself to help the children play co-operatively. (Try to avoid imposing too many of your own ideas upon the group!)

For older children
Suggest that they may wish to write an account of a real or imaginary trip to an airport for others to read and enjoy.

Follow-up activities
● Visit an airport viewing gallery.
● Make your own passports, using a real photograph or a self-portrait for identification.
● Set up an airport area with suitcases, check-in desks, a café and passport control.
● Make junk model aircraft and paint them realistically.

WHO AM I?

Learning objective
To find out about farms, farm animals and their young.

Group size
Up to six children.

What you need
A set of farm animals, model buildings or cardboard boxes, green, yellow and brown paper, masking tape, felt-tipped pens, foil, adhesive, Plasticine, tiny dry twigs, play people and farm vehicles. Books, posters, stories and pictures of farms and farm animals.

Setting up
Cover a table with the coloured paper in sections to represent fields, holding them securely into place with masking tape. Draw roads and pathways and add a foil pond. Push twigs into blobs of Plasticine to make model trees and set out the buildings for the animals and people. Set up an area nearby in which to display the literature for the children to investigate.

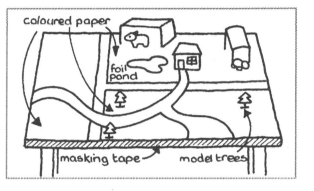

What to do

Invite the children to play with the farm and to share the books and pictures with an adult as well as each other. Then gather the group together to play the game. Tell the children you are going to think of an animal and give them clues to see if they can guess what it is. Ask them to close their eyes while you select an animal to hide behind your back. When someone guesses correctly reinforce this by showing them the hidden animal. Older children should be able to take turns as clue givers but younger children may need help.

Questions to ask
I am a little woolly animal and when I grow up I will be a sheep. What am I? I used to be a foal but now I have grown up. What am I? My daddy was a boar and my mummy was a sow. What am I? I am a calf and my mummy was a cow. What was my daddy? My mummy says, 'Quack, quack'. What am I? A chicken laid an egg and I hatched out. What am I?

For younger children
Help the children by making the sounds of the animals as clues. If necessary let younger children work together to guess the animals.

For older children
Encourage older children to use their acquired knowledge to give 'clever clues' for the other children For example, they could say 'I have trotters and a snout', or 'I am a mare's baby', as clues.

Follow-up activities
● Make a 'Mummies and babies' book with as many different animals as you can.
● Make a large number farm collage with, for example, six cows, five hens, four ducks, three pigs, two sheep and one horse.
● Sing 'Old MacDonald'.
● Visit a working farm or a farm park.

HOSPITALS

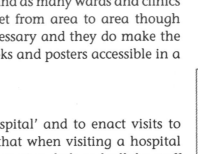

Learning objective
To investigate health care and how to keep healthy.

Group size
Up to six children.

What you need
Several open-topped cardboard boxes, play people and accessories (commercially produced or home-made), ambulances, books, posters and stories about hospitals.

Setting up
Arrange the boxes to form the ground floor of a hospital, putting in furniture and accessories as necessary to make a casualty department, a reception area, an operating theatre and as many wards and clinics as you like. (Doors can be made to get from area to area though young children often find these unnecessary and they do make the structure less adaptable.) Have the books and posters accessible in a corner nearby.

What to do
Invite the group to play with the 'hospital' and to enact visits to hospital for various reasons. Explain that when visiting a hospital you normally have to check in at the reception desk and tell the staff why you have come. Suggest that you, the adult, could perhaps play the part of the receptionist so that you can write down all the reasons in a special book. (In this way you will be able to extend their play in a non-intrusive manner, supplying and explaining such words as *consultant* and *x-ray* in order to expand their vocabulary naturally.)

Questions to ask
Why might we visit a hospital? (Because we have had an accident/need a check up/need an operation/are having a baby/are visiting a patient/have suddenly become ill.) Who looks after us in hospital? (Doctors and nurses.) How do very sick people get to hospital? (In an ambulance.)

For younger children
Introduce the play session by sharing some books and talking about hospitals to provide some starting points.

For older children
Encourage them to take the part of the receptionist themselves and make their own notes.

Follow-up activities
● Turn the home corner into a hospital/eye clinic/baby clinic.
● Make some posters telling people how to keep healthy, for example always brush your teeth, take plenty of exercise, eat fruit and vegetables instead of sweets and crisps.
● Invite a local dentist in to talk about keeping your teeth healthy.
● Suggest a 'Healthy Eating Challenge' and try to eat no crisps, chocolate or sweets for a whole week.

WHERE WE LIVE

Learning objective
To make, talk about and record detailed observations.

Group size
Up to four children.

What you need
Boxes, adhesive, card offcuts, kitchen paper, felt-tipped pens, paints, scissors, (a Polaroid camera would be useful though not essential), notepads and pencils.

Setting up
Take a short walk around the locality or merely stand outside and observe any houses within view. Notice the different types of windows and doors. Look for any patterns such as brickwork or roofs. Take photographs if possible, or ask the children to draw on the notepads any details they want to remember.

What to do
Back indoors invite the children to cover the boxes with kitchen paper to make houses and to add roofs made from cardboard. While the adhesive is drying on the models, ask the group to look at the photographs and their notepads and to try to recall the details of the houses they saw.

Using the available materials ask the children to recreate some of the details they have seen on their own models. Once these are completed and dry compare them to the photographs or go back outside and compare them with the houses you looked at originally.

Questions to ask
How many different shaped windows are there? What shapes are they? What about the doors? How many chimneys are on the house? Are the houses terraced, semi-detached or detached? Are there any bungalows? Do the doors have numbers on? Do they have letter boxes? Do they have any glass in them?

For younger children
Choose just two details to concentrate on. For example: how many windows are there? What colour is the front door?

For older children
While outside, encourage older children to jot down or draw as many details as possible of their chosen house so that they can produce it as accurately as possible on their model.

Follow-up activities
● Put all the houses in a row and populate them with suitable sized play people.
● Read and act out the story of 'The Three Little Pigs'.
● Mix some sand and paint together to make textured paint for the walls of your house.
● Make up a short story about the people who live in your model house.

GARAGES

Learning objective
To use skills such as cutting, folding and choosing materials for a given purpose.

Group size
Up to six children.

What you need
Reclaimed materials – including variously sized boxes and cardboard, scissors, adhesive, large paper fasteners, awl, masking tape, model vehicles of differing sizes.

Setting up
Walk around the local area to look particularly at garages and their doors. Point out any interesting details and ask plenty of questions to ensure the children observe carefully. If you meet any friendly neighbours perhaps they would show you how their garage doors open and close. Once back indoors, invite each child to select a vehicle from those available.

What to do
Ask the children to construct a suitable garage for their chosen vehicle, making sure it is the right size – neither too big nor too small – and has a door or doors that open and close. Show them a paper fastener, and demonstrate how it makes a handle that they might find useful on their doors.

Once the children know what they have to do, stand back and allow them to select their own materials and make their constructions. Be ready to supply tools, equipment or advice as necessary, and use the awl if the children need to make holes for paper fasteners.

back of door

head of fastener acts as turning door knob

fasteners jut from door edge to make a latch which catches on door frame and keeps door closed (or behind 2nd door)

head of fastener can also provide a non-turning handle for lifting open an "up and over" door.

Questions to ask
Is your garage going to fit your vehicle? How can you tell? (The vehicle has been put inside or measured against it.) Which way will the door open? (Upwards or sideways.) Will the door stay closed? If not, what might you do to change this? (Put on a latch of some sort.)

For younger children
They may need adult help to cut the boxes if they are of thick cardboard.

For older children
Help them to add batteries, wires, switches and bulbs so that a light may be fitted inside each garage.

Follow-up activities
● Number the garages and vehicles and use them for number matching activities.
● Do a survey to find the most popular colour of car belonging to children's families in the group. Display the results as a pictograph.
● Sort the garages and/or the vehicles into ascending/descending order of length.
● Sing 'The wheels of the car go round and round', making up your own verses, for example 'The seatbelts in the car go click, click, click'; 'The petrol in the car goes glug, glug, glug' and so on.

Glue

Use large movements in 'Musical vehicles' and fine motor skills in 'Articulated play figures' to develop all the children's physical skills. This chapter provides a range of practical activities to fine tune the children's increasing body control.

ANIMAL ROUNDABOUT

Learning objective
To use controlled movement to imitate animals.

Group size
Eight children.

What you need
A bag containing at least eight different play animals.

Setting up
With the children, look at the animals individually and discuss their similarities and differences. Concentrate particularly on how they move. Replace the animals in the bag.

What to do
Arrange the children in a circle so that they are about five metres away from each another. Ask one child to dip a hand into the bag, select an animal and then move like the animal which has been picked out towards the next child in the circle. That child then dips into the bag and moves like the chosen animal to the next child and so on around the circle until all the children have had a turn or until the bag is empty.

Questions to ask
How does the chosen animal move? Does it plod, creep or jump? Does it move on two hind legs or does it travel on all fours? Does it go slowly or quickly? Does it move silently or is it likely to be noisy? If it makes a noise, what sort of a noise is it? Is it a heavy animal or is it light?

For younger children
Practise the various animal movements altogether as a whole group before playing the roundabout game.

For older children
When a child chooses an animal make sure nobody else can see what animal has been picked out. The next child must guess from the movements which animal is being portrayed.

Follow-up activities
● Visit a zoo or a pet shop and carefully observe the movement of a variety of animals.
● Make a collection of words to describe different ways of moving – creep, slither, crawl, swing, clamber and lope.
● Sort a set of toy animals according to how they move.
● Read or tell the story of Noah's Ark.

ARTICULATED PLAY FIGURES

What you need
Photocopiable page 63 – two copies for each child, stiff paper or thin card, scissors, adhesive, cardboard tubes about 12cm long, awl and split pins.

Setting up
Make a sample figure yourself. If you have access to a photocopier which will take thin card, copy the activity sheet directly onto the card, otherwise, stick copies onto the card so that they will be dry for the children to use.

What to do
Encourage each child to cut out the pieces on their sheets – only one head is needed! – making sure to keep them all safe as they go along. (Some children may find it easier to join the sections together as they are done.) Demonstrate how to manipulate split pins (CARE! – most children will be able to manage this for themselves though some may require a little help to start them off.) Assemble the pieces around the cardboard tubes. Let the children practise moving their completed model, bending the limbs to 'walk' along.

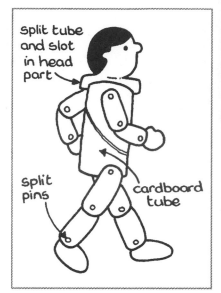

split tube and slot in head part

split pins

cardboard tube

Questions to ask
Encourage the children to talk about the models as they are working. Do they know all the body parts they are cutting out? Can they find those parts on their own bodies? Do they know the names of the joints? Are there any more joints we have not put into the models? (Fingers, toes, neck, jaw and so on.)

For younger children
A simplified model could be made by doing away with some of the joints. Very young children will need considerable help with the cutting out.

For older children
Under extremely close supervision, older children may be allowed to use the awl themselves. Demonstrate how to do this safely by placing Blu-Tack or Plasticine under the object being pierced. Always keep the awl safely out of reach when not in use. Let them make up short plays using their models.

Follow-up activities
● Use the figures for the action game on page 45.
● Put the figure into various poses and use it as a still-life model for stick-people sketches.
● Devise a sequence of movements for your figure and ask a friend to copy them.
● Collect as many action words as you can and try to make your figure do them – run, jump, swim, hop, march, tip-toe and so on.

ACTION GAMES

Learning objective
To practise running, jumping, hopping and crawling.

Group size
Up to 20 children.

What you need
Articulated play figures (commercially produced or home-made – see page 44), empty cardboard boxes and a large open space.

Setting up
Put each play figure into a pose showing a different movement such as running, jumping, crawling or hopping and hide it under a box. Then use another play figure to demonstrate the different positions it can be put into and discuss the movements depicted by each pose.

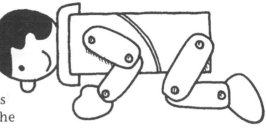

What to do
When the children are thoroughly familiar with the various poses and which movements they are showing, invite a child to choose a box which can be lifted to reveal a figure posed to depict a particular movement. The children must then decide which movement is being demonstrated and try to do that movement themselves either for a set length of time perhaps for 30 seconds, or to a given destination such as from one side of the room/playground to the other.

Remind the children that they must look where they are going the whole time so as not to bump into other people. Let the children take it in turns to reveal different figures and to copy the movement, until all of the models have been revealed.

Questions to ask
What action is the figure portraying? Which parts of its body are touching the floor? How is the rest of its body held? Has it got straight arms or bent arms, raised arms or lowered arms? Point out that the play figure always looks forward so that it can see where it is going. Does it appear to be going fast or slow? How can you tell? (It may be leaning forward when in a running position.)

For younger children
It may be necessary to insist that they all travel in the same direction as one another to avoid crashes if they have little space awareness.

For older children
Put the figures into increasingly complex poses to depict more imaginative ways of moving and to necessitate extremely careful observation. For example: tiptoeing with one arm raised and bent and the other arm straight and lowered, or sliding on the back with legs raised and arms bent.

Follow-up activities
● Use two play figures to move together for pairs of children to imitate.
● Look at a skeleton to see how its joints work.
● Read stories from the *Funny Bones* series of books by Allan Ahlberg (Mammoth Books).
● Sing 'Heads, shoulders, knees and toes'.

PENALTY SHOTS

Learning objective
To practise controlled
and accurate
movements.

Group size
Up to six children.

What you need
Seven play people, a black felt-tipped pen, a marble-sized ball of Plasticine or Blu-Tack and a shoe box.

Setting up
Cut out one long side of the shoe box and draw a grid of lines on all remaining sides to represent netting. Stand the box on its open side as a goal.

What to do
Choose one child to pick a play figure and to be the goalkeeper. The remaining five children then choose a figure and take turns to try to score a goal by making their player kick the ball past the goalkeeper. (At this stage do not fix a penalty spot to shoot from.) Keep scores for them while they each have three turns.

After a few turns, one of the children will probably place their ball very close to the goal to take their shot. This will lead to a discussion about fairness which, in turn, will lead to the fixing of the penalty spot. In this way the children will appreciate the need for a fixed spot, rather than simply being told at the beginning of the game that there is one. Select a new goalkeeper and play again and continue until everyone has had a turn at being goalkeeper.

Questions to ask
What happens if the ball is kicked too softly? (It stops before it reaches the goal.) What happens if you try to kick it too hard? (It sometimes makes the play figure's legs bend backwards so it is not a proper kick.) How can you stop the legs bending backwards? (Hold the figure sideways on to the ball.) When is it easy for the goalkeeper to stop the ball? (When the ball travels slowly in a straight line.) When is it more difficult? (When the ball goes very fast.)

For younger children
Use larger tennis or sponge balls and teddy bears or dolls instead of play figures and make a larger goal.

For older children
Experiment with different materials to make a ball that is lighter and therefore less earthbound.

Follow-up activities
● Hold a real penalty tournament outside using a real football goal.
● Practise all sorts of ball skills such as dribbling, bouncing, throwing, catching and rolling.
● Think of as many ball games as you can – from piggy-in-the-middle to tenpin bowling.
● Design a football strip, using two colours of your own choice.

CAR MAKING

Learning objective
To experience the qualities of papier mâché.

Group size
Up to four children.

What you need
Newspapers, large bowl or bucket of water, four smaller bowls or basins, paper glue (Gloy or similar), protective aprons, drinking straws, petroleum jelly, card discs, paint.

Setting up
Ask the children to tear the newspaper into strips of 2cm or less and then into small squares. Put these to soak in the bucket of water for at least 24 hours.

What to do
Drain off the excess water. Press the pulp hard and drain again. (It should be well-soaked but not dripping.) Give each child a bowl and at least two large handfuls of squeezed pulp. Then ask them to break up the pulp, pulling it apart to see if there are any large pieces of paper still intact. If there are, they should be torn smaller. Once this is done, add a handful of paste to each bowl for the children to squeeze, pull, push and pat for as long as possible to produce a smooth mâché which can then be moulded into a simple car shape.

To make axles, coat drinking straws in petroleum jelly (CARE!) – and push them through the mâché in the desired places. Leave to dry in a warm, airy place for several days. The models can then be painted and card disc wheels finally added to make quite sturdy, but not waterproof, toy cars.

Follow-up activities
● Use other materials to make cars – Plasticine, play dough, clay, reclaimed materials, construction toys, paper – to build an interesting display.
● Cut out pictures from magazines and brochures to make a colourful car collage.
● Go for a walk and see how many different letters of the alphabet you can spot in car numbers.

Questions to ask
What happens to your hands as you tear the paper? (They become black.) Why? (The ink stains them.) What happens to the words on the wet newspaper as it is squeezed and prodded? (They begin to disappear and the mixture turns grey.) What does it feel like when the paste is added? (Cold, slimy, squidgy, squashy.) What happens to the mâché as it dries out? (It becomes hard and lighter – both in its colour and weight.)

For younger children
Have a supplementary supply of shredded newspaper to soak since very young children tend to forget to tear tiny enough pieces.

For older children
Use toy cars as models to copy and encourage them to mould details such as headlights, bumper bars and spoilers.

OBSTACLE COURSE

Learning objective
To handle a range of materials to complete a given task.

Group size
Up to four children.

What you need
A variety of construction toys (Duplo, LEGO, wooden bricks, Brio) string, netting, a few jointed dolls or home-made play figures (see page 44). Pictures of children engaged in outdoor activities.

Setting up
Ask the children if they know what an obstacle course is. (They may have seen obstacle races at sports days.) Suggest that it might be fun to build a course for the play figures to follow. Make a list of the sort of equipment they would like to make, offering suggestions and showing pictures if necessary.

What to do
Suggest that different children make different pieces of equipment. Help them to sort through the available materials and to decide who is making what. Allow the children to solve their own design problems as much as possible, offering suggestions and practical help only when absolutely necessary. Encourage them to consider such things as the strength and stability of their constructions. Help the children to lay out their finished pieces of equipment like an obstacle course. Allow them some free play with the play figures.

Questions to ask
How is this piece of equipment to be used? Which part of the body does it exercise the most? Is it large and strong enough to suit the doll? (Test it to see.) In which order should the different items be placed on the course? Should a scramble net be followed by a steep upward incline? (No, because they are both hard work for the legs.)

For younger children
Cardboard boxes make a useful addition to the smaller construction materials.

For older children
Encourage them to plan and design the course on paper before beginning co-operative construction work.

Follow-up activities
● Construct a simple and safe obstacle course for yourself and your friends.
● Using construction toys or reclaimed materials, design an exercise machine and explain how it works.
● Read *A Piece of Cake* by Jill Murphy (Walker Books).
● Devise a sequence of four different exercises and try to perform it three times.

COPY-CAT FUN

Learning objective
To move confidently with increasing control and co-ordination.

Group size
Up to 20 children.

What you need
A string puppet person and a string puppet animal.

Setting up
Introduce each toy to the group and discuss how it moves, paying particular attention to its joints.

What to do
Select one of the toys and place it in a sitting position. Ask the children to look carefully at the toy and to notice how it is sitting. Challenge them to sit the same way, checking the position of their arms, legs, heads and backs. Now slowly make the toy rise into a standing position, while the children observe closely and try to copy the actions. Then move the toy's limbs in a walking motion for the children to imitate.

Try many other movements, both large and small, such as nodding the head, waving a hand, stretching on tiptoe or falling into a crumpled heap. Once they are familiar with these movements, repeat the activity with the second puppet, encouraging the children to think about how the different movements and positions feel.

Questions to ask
Does the puppet person have elbows and knees? Do they bend the same way as ours do? What about the animal puppet? (Although it has four legs its joints probably bend backwards more like our elbows than our knees.) Is it possible to stand up without bending either your arms or your legs? What does it feel like to walk with straight arms and legs? Is it possible to run with straight legs?

For younger children
Talk them through their actions as they move, helping them to become more aware of their bodies and how they are moving, and to reinforce the 'body' vocabulary.

For older children
Invent music to depict the various movements of each toy and to create a group 'Puppet dance'.

Follow-up activities
● Spend ten minutes trying to do normal activities with straight arms or straight legs and record some that are very difficult (such as having a drink) and some that are relatively easy (such as reading a book).
● Take a look at some other toys and dolls and try to move like them.
● Watch a professional puppeteer using string puppets and notice how they work.
● Convert a soft toy into a string puppet by fixing thread from its head, hands and feet to a pair of crossed sticks.

MUSICAL VEHICLES

Learning objective
To use music as a stimulus to movement and to become aware of space.

Group size
Six to 20 children.

What you need
A toy boat, train, aeroplane and bicycle, a large open space, a source of music.

Setting up
Decide upon a suitable action to represent each toy for example sitting and rowing for the boat, shuffling and moving the arms for the train; running with outstretched arms for the aeroplane; and lying and pedalling legs for the bicycle. Familiarise the children with these actions and ensure they know which vehicle they represent.

What to do
Explain that you are going to show the children a vehicle and then play some music. While the music plays, they must do the action to go with that vehicle. When the music stops they must stop and look out for the next vehicle to be shown and so on.

Play the music for varying lengths of time and vary the order in which you present the vehicles. Remind the children to watch where they are going and to try to use all the space available, even the corners, trying not to bump into one another.

Questions to ask
Why is it important to listen while you move? (So you can hear when the music stops.) And why is it important to look at the adult when you stop moving? (So you know which vehicle is coming next.) Can you make your aeroplane swoop low? Can you drive your car slowly? Can you pedal your bicycle backwards? Can you make your train whistle occasionally too?

Follow-up activities
● Sort a set of vehicles into land, sea and air types.
● Make a paper aeroplane and see how far it can fly.
● Look at a map and try to spot roads, rivers and railways. Then draw a map of your own showing the same features.
● Do a traffic survey and record how many bicycles, cars, vans, buses and lorries go by.

For younger children
Some very young children can be overwhelmed by the boisterous nature of this activity and they may need considerable support and encouragement to join in.

For older children
Suggest that the train should consist of at least three children and that the boat should be rowed by two children sitting facing one another and holding hands.

Encourage your children to develop all their senses in this chapter with practical ideas to explore sound, art work and touch. Using a range of materials the children can make a dolls' house and do some printing using small world toys.

TRAFFIC RHYTHMS

Learning objective
To explore rhythmic sounds.

Group size
Up to 20 children.

What you need
A selection of toy vehicles – one for each child, a copy of photocopiable page 64 (enlarged if possible).

Setting up
Look at each type of vehicle in turn and discuss the sounds they could make together. Decide on an appropriate sound of your own for each vehicle or use the list below.

What to do
Hand out a vehicle to each child and then ask the children to group themselves according to the vehicle they have, so that all the cars are together and all the aeroplanes are together and so on. Explain that you are going to try to work together to make some traffic music. Go through the vehicles again in turn and practise the sounds for each, saying them in a lively, rhythmic manner. For example:

motorbike – vroOOom
aeroplane – nye-ow
train – choo-choo
boat – splash
car – beep-be-beep

Encourage the children to spin the wheels or tap their vehicle in time with the sounds. Now ask them to make the sound of their vehicle every time you point to their group, but at no other time. Using photocopiable page 64, or sequences of your own, conduct the groups by pointing to them in repetitive order.

Questions to ask
What happens if children make their sounds at the wrong time? (It spoils the pattern or rhythm that is being created.) Can the children hear where the pattern begins its repeat? Can they anticipate which sound is coming next even before you point to them?

For younger children
Work with a maximum of six children at first, using very simple sequences and perhaps only two sounds to begin with.

For older children
Allow plenty of time for individuals as well as groups to experiment with the sounds, varying pitch, timing and volume to create an extensive repertoire.

Follow-up activities
● Use the vehicles to start a 'sound box' for free experimentation, adding various everyday objects to extend the range of sounds.
● Invent some symbols so that the music can be written down for others to follow.
● Clap the rhythm of well-known nursery rhymes for the children to guess.
● Invite a musician in to play for you.

SIZE PROBLEMS

Learning objective
To use imaginative and creative thinking to consider relative size.

Group size
Up to 20 children.

What you need
A small doll.

Setting up
Consider the size of the doll in relation to the children, the furniture and other everyday objects. Ask the children to imagine what it would be like to be as small as the doll. Discuss some of the advantages and disadvantages of being that size.

What to do
Ask the children to sit in a circle with you in the centre holding the doll. Explain to the group that you are going to take turns to think about what it might be like to be as small as a doll. Start the game by saying, 'If I was as small as the doll I wonder how I could get into my bed.' or 'I wonder what it would be like to meet a dog.' Invite ideas and suggestions from the children and discuss their ideas in turn. Find a volunteer to take your place with the doll in the centre of the circle to continue with another problem to be solved by the group – or another situation to think about. Encourage the children to expand their ideas to achieve solutions, for example if a child suggests you would need a smaller bed, ask 'how would you make a bed, what materials would you need, and what height and length ought it to be?'.

Questions to ask
Why might it be frightening to meet a dog? (Because it will be much bigger than you.) What might happen if you tried to run away? (It might chase you.) Is there anything else you could do instead of running away? (Try and make friends with it.) How? (By keeping still and talking gently to it.) If you became friends with the dog what might happen next? (It might give you a ride on its back or invite you into its kennel.)

For younger children
Work in groups of only three or four children so that everyone can contribute.

For older children
Suggest that they might use one of the situations as the basis of a story to write, draw or tell.

Follow-up activities
● Read *Mrs Pepperpot Stories* by Alf Proysen (Red Fox).
● Design and/or make something to help a tiny person to climb onto a full-sized chair.
● Act out the story of *The Three Bears*.
● Make a collection of things small enough to fit in a matchbox.

GUESS WHAT?

Learning objective
To use both touch and
sight to make
deductions about given
objects.

Group size
Up to 15 children.

What you need
Six identical pairs of small world toys – vehicles/people/furniture, a cardboard box, a small square of fabric, sticky tape.

Setting up
Cut a hole in the side of the box, big enough for a child's hand to fit through. Affix the fabric to the inside of the box to curtain the hole.

What to do
Choose six children to stand at the front of the group and give each child a different toy to hold. Put the remaining six matching toys into the box and invite a child from the remainder of the group to feel in the box and find a particular toy.

At first, the children at the front can keep their toys visible throughout the game. Once the children are familiar with the procedure they can hide the toys behind their backs as soon as a child has been told which toy to pick out. This will encourage the child to keep the image of the toy in mind while feeling in the box. When the selection has been made, the child at the front can reveal the matching item. The game continues with children taking turns both at the front and feeling in the box until they have all had a turn at both activities.

Questions to ask
Encourage the children to describe what they can feel in the box. Does it feel hard or soft? Are there any moving parts? Is it rough, smooth, crinkly or bumpy? Does it fit right inside your hand or is it too big for that? From what has been described does the group think the right toy has been chosen?

For younger children
Make two holes in the box so that the children can easily put both hands into the box in order to feel the objects.

For older children
Invite one child to stand at the front and one to stand by the box. The child at the front can secretly choose one of the six toys, keep it hidden from view and then give two or three clues to the other child who can feel in the box and select the matching toy.

Follow-up activities
● Use non-identical pairs of toys such as cup/saucer; train/track; fireman/ladder and doll/dress for example.
● Play 'Blind Man's Buff' and try to guess who you have caught by touch alone.
● Make a series of covered feely boxes using ice-cream tubs containing cooked spaghetti, flour and water, dried leaves, ice-cubes, half-set jelly and so on.
● Contact the Royal National Institute for the Blind and find out all you can about Braille, raised watch faces and other useful items.

I CAN DRAW

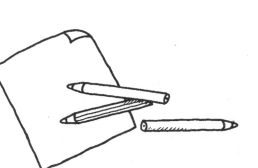

Learning objective
To develop close
observation and
attention to detail in
drawing.

Group size
Up to six children.

What you need
A variety of paper, pens and pencils for drawing, a selection of play figures, puppets or dolls.

Setting up
Ask each child to select a particular toy to look at.

What to do
Invite the children to choose a piece of paper and some pens or pencils for drawing. Ask them to place their chosen toy on the table in front of them and to look at it very carefully. Allow them to position the toy whichever way they choose. Then ask them to draw the toy as accurately as possible, so that other people may later be able to guess who drew which toy. Encourage them to look carefully at the colour of their toy as well as its overall shape. Remind them to think about the positions of arms or legs and to look carefully at any facial features.

Questions to ask
Have you looked really carefully at all the little details of your toy? Is it the same colour all over? Are the arms and legs the same size as one another? Are they jointed – and if they are, which way do they bend? Does the toy have a neck? Does it have fingers or even toes?

For younger children
You may need to talk very young children through their drawings to continually remind them of the task in hand.

For older children
Encourage them to lightly sketch with a pencil before using coloured pens or crayons.

Follow-up activities
● Visit a gallery to look at some famous still-life paintings and notice how much detail is included.
● Display the finished pictures alongside the real toys for comparison.
● Pin interesting swatches of fabric to the corners of paper for the children to try to copy. Invite them to mix colours to match it.
● Ask the children to paint a picture of the clothes that somebody in the group is wearing and see if their friends can guess whose clothes they are.

VEGETABLE ZOO

Learning objective
To create zoo animals from vegetables for a small world zoo.

Group size
Up to six children.

What you need
A selection of vegetables, cardboard discs, offcuts of paper, card and fabrics of various textures, buttons, drinking straws, wool, feathers, strong adhesive or double-sided tape, felt-tipped pens, blunted cocktail sticks, de-headed match sticks, or small pieces of thin dowelling, play figures and toy fences or cages.

Setting up
Show the children each vegetable in turn, naming and discussing it. Explore the way the vegetables smell, look and feel. CARE! – remind the children that some vegetables should not be eaten raw, so they should never put anything in their mouths unless an adult has told them it is safe to do so.

What to do
Suggest that it might be fun to make a zoo full of different animals made from vegetables! Invite each child to choose a vegetable as a base, supply all the craft materials suggested above and stand back and allow the children to create their own creatures. Try not to intervene unless really necessary, allowing the children to test their ideas and learn from their mistakes as they go along.

When the models are complete, add play figures and fences to make the vegetable creatures ready for imaginative play.

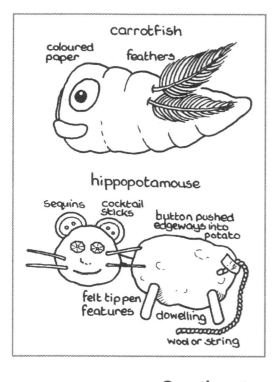

carrotfish

coloured paper

feathers

hippopotamouse

sequins   cocktail sticks

button pushed edgeways into potato

felt tip pen features

dowelling

wool or string

Follow-up activities
● Repeat the activity using fruit instead of vegetables.
● Do some vegetable printing.
● Make some vegetable soup.
● Turn the home corner into a greengrocer's shop.

Questions to ask
Is your animal going to have a head and a body? How might you join two vegetables together? (With the straws or sticks perhaps.) Do you notice anything about the vegetables when their skin is pierced? (Some may begin to seep juice or stain the fingers, others may begin to smell more strongly.)

For younger children
Prepare some features such as eyes, ears, noses, beaks and tails, to start them off.

For older children
Name their creatures after themselves – perhaps a Paulephant or a Sallypotamus – and suggest where the creatures might live or what they might eat.

MAKING A DOLLS' HOUSE

Learning objective
To use a range of textured materials to make an open-sided dolls' house.

Group size
Up to four children.

What you need
Four cardboard boxes, cardboard, masking tape, adhesive, offcuts of various types of carpet, fabrics, floor and wall-coverings, paint and scissors.

Setting up
Tell the children that they are each going to make a different room and then join them all together to make a house. Decide who is going to make which room.

Remove the box lids and one adjacent side leaving a structure with top, bottom, two closed sides and two open sides.

What to do
Invite the children to select a suitable floor-covering for their particular room, plus a wall-covering for the two walls. Encourage them to measure the required materials, cut them out and stick them into place.

Once all four rooms are complete, ask the children how the rooms might fit together to make a house. They can then each spread adhesive on the outside of the right hand wall of their room and push them together to make an open-sided house. Strengthen the structure by sealing top and base seams with masking tape. Now paint black stripes on the top of the building to represent rafters. Finally, make a roof by folding a piece of strong card in half, attaching it to the house with masking tape along the edges and asking the children to paint it.

Questions to ask
Sometimes walls and floors need to be washable or easy to wipe clean, ask the children why they think this might be. (Because there may be babies or young children in the house or things might get spilt.) Which rooms might get dirtier or wetter than others? (Kitchen and bathroom.) Why do they think this is? Which rooms might want soft warm carpets? (Bedroom and lounge.)

For younger children
You may need to help younger children to cut out the fabrics to the correct size.

For older children
Older children can develop their houses by adding a loft hole, or a second storey for which they could also construct a staircase for access to it.

Follow-up activities
● Make some furniture and populate your house with pipe-cleaner people.
● Investigate various floor and wall-coverings in your own home and discuss your findings with your friends.
● Go for a walk and look at different sorts of houses – terraced, semi-detached and bungalows for example.

LASTING IMPRESSIONS

Learning objective
To make plaster models from Plasticine moulds.

Group size
Up to six children.

What you need
Plaster of Paris, Plasticine, simple play figures or vehicles.

Setting up
Try this activity yourself before trying it with the children so you know what to expect.

What to do
Give each child a lump of Plasticine about the size of a tennis ball and ask them to make it into a smooth ball with no cracks in. Then ask them to choose one of the toys to press down into the Plasticine – face down or wheels uppermost – until it is level with, or slightly below the surface. Then carefully remove the toy without disturbing the mould.

Mix the plaster of Paris while the children watch. (Take care not to create bubbles in the mixture as you stir but work quite quickly because the plaster will begin to set almost immediately.) Pour the plaster into the mould and leave the casts to set thoroughly before inviting the children to carefully peel away the Plasticine to leave a plaster model of their chosen toy.

Questions to ask
The plaster of Paris was a powder to begin with, but what happened when the water was added? (The powder dissolved and it turned into a thin paste.) What had happened when you came back later? (It had set hard to make a solid.) What happens if you gently scrape the back of your model? (Powder falls from it.) What happens if you gently scrape the edge of your model against some dark paper? (It leaves a white mark like chalk.) What happens to chalk when it gets wet? (It crumbles and dissolves.) So what might happen to your model if it gets wet? (The same thing!)

For younger children
They may need help to remove their toy from the Plasticine without disturbing the mould.

For older children
The models can be decorated with paints or felt-tipped pens and varnished for a more lasting finish.

Follow-up activities
● Investigate the difference between dissolving and melting.
● Try to find ten different solids and ten different liquids.
● Make a solid plaster block, using a yoghurt pot as a mould and use sandpaper to sculpt it into shape.
● Visit a gallery to look at the work of professional sculptors.

UNUSUAL PRINTS

Learning objective
To investigate off-set printing using small world toys.

Group size
Up to four children.

What you need
Poster paint, brushes, selection of small world toys, old newspapers, white paper and foam sponges.

Setting up
This can be a very messy activity so make sure all surfaces are well-protected and have a bowl of warm soapy water ready for hand-washing. Make sure the toys used are either old or paint- and waterproof.

What to do
Give each child a piece of clean white paper and allow them to each choose a toy. Tell them to place their toy on a sheet of newspaper and to cover all its visible surfaces in paint. When it's covered, show them how to press a foam sponge evenly down on top of the toy to pick up the print. They can then press the sponge down onto the clean white paper to transfer the print. Repeat the process using different toys to build up an interesting picture. Try using different surfaces of the toys for different effects.

Questions to ask
Is it possible to make a print by just pressing the paint-covered toy onto the paper? (Let the children try it to see.) Why is it possible with the sponge then? (Because the sponge wraps itself around the toy to pick up paint from all the surfaces.) What happens if you spend too long coating the toy with paint? (The paint dries out before you can take a print.) What happens if you move the sponge as you press it onto the toy? (It smudges and does not give a clear print.)

For younger children
Using small pieces of sponge, rather than brushes, to cover the toy with paint may help give a quicker and more even finish.

For older children
Use sponge paint rollers to roll a print off the toys.

Follow-up activities
● Experiment with other 3-D objects to get some unusual prints for your friends to guess.
● Try to pick up prints from 3-D objects with other materials – foam pipe-lagging, kitchen roll paper or paper handkerchiefs.
● Experiment with different coloured paper and paints.
● Print your own wallpaper to use in shoe box houses (page 56).

PHOTOCOPIABLES

Name _____

Colour Humpty, stick him onto some card. Draw on lines to make six pieces. Cut the pieces out to make a puzzle.

Name _____

Cut out and stick the pictures into the correct room.

bathroom

bedroom

kitchen

lounge/dining room

Name _____

Colour the pieces then cut them out to build your nativity figure.

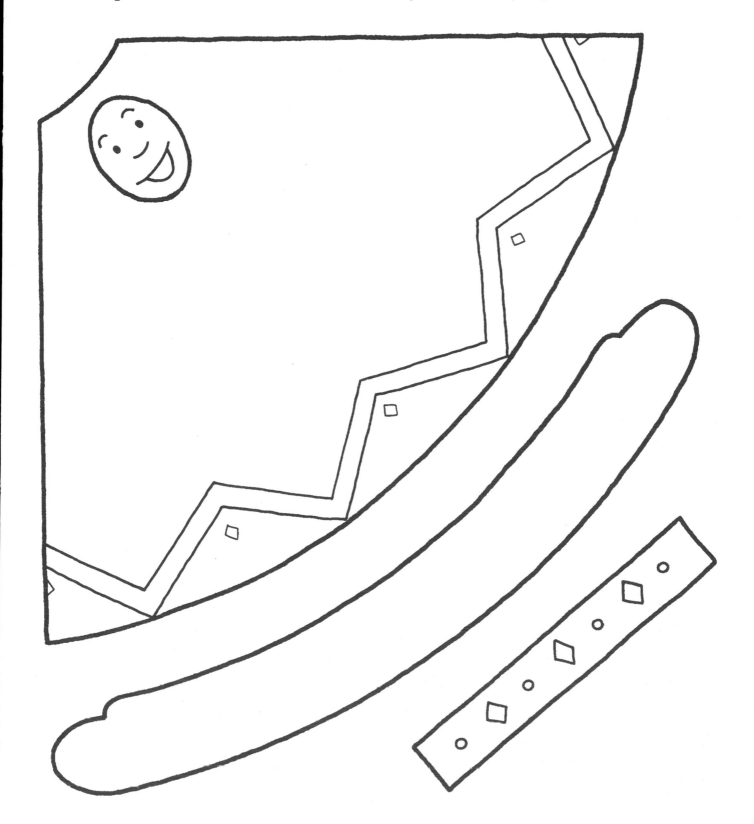

Name _____

Draw safe routes from the house – in red to the church, in blue to
the park, in black to the toy shop and in green to the swimming pool.

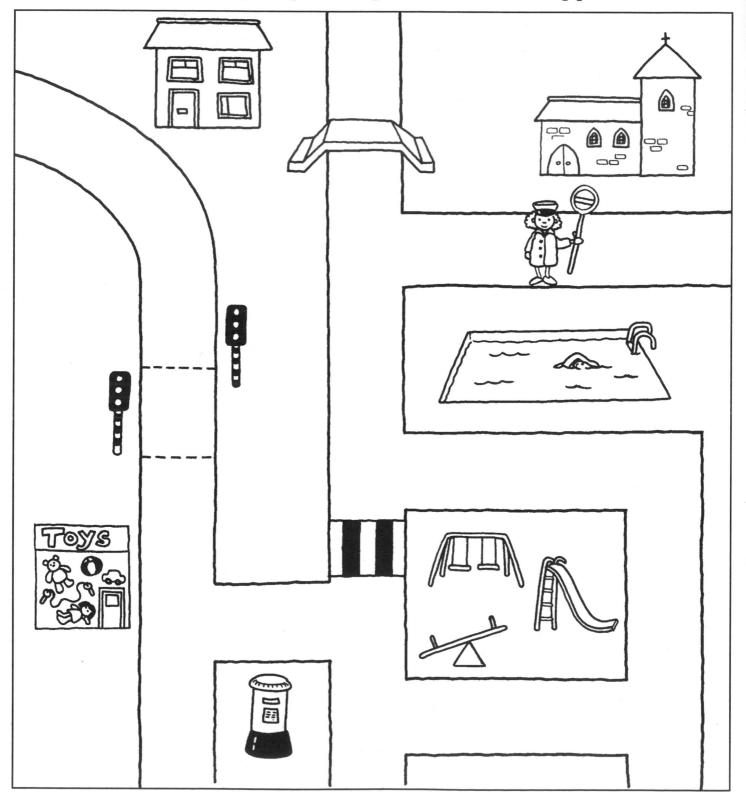

Name _____

Stick or photocopy two copies on to thin card or stiff paper, cut out the pieces along the **bold** lines and assemble with paper fasteners to make jointed people.

Name _____

Chant each line several times to make four individual rhythm patterns.

Line 1

| choo-choo | beep-be-beep | vroOOom | splash |

Line 2

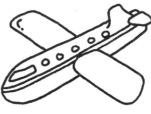

| nye-ow | nye-ow | nye-ow | choo-choo |

Line 3

| choo-choo | nye-ow | beep-be-beep | vroOOom |

Line 4

| beep-be-beep | splash | vroOOom | splash |

Then use them in various combinations to produce more complex patterns.